Maharishi Pat
Yoga Sūtra

translated by

Thomas Egenes, Ph.D.

1st WORLD LIBRARY
Literary Society

Maharishi Patañjali Yoga Sūtra

Thomas Egenes, Ph.D.

Published by 1st World Publishing
P.O. Box 2211, Fairfield, Iowa 52556
tel: 641-209-5000 • fax: 866-440-5234
web: www.1stworldpublishing.com

First Edition

LCCN: 2009936296

SoftCover ISBN: 978-1-4218-9132-3

HardCover ISBN: 978-1-4218-9131-6

eBook ISBN: 978-1-4218-9133-0

This material has been written and published solely for educational purposes. The author and the publisher shall have neither liability nor responsibility to any person or entity with respect to any loss, damage or injury caused or alleged to be caused directly or indirectly by the information contained in this book.

The characters and events described in this text are intended to entertain and teach rather than present an exact factual history of real people or events.

Front cover photograph by Sankari Wegman
Back cover photograph by Brandy Lee-Jacob
Cover design by Lawrence Sheaff

With gratitude to

His Holiness Maharishi Mahesh Yogi,

who brought to light the full meaning of the Yoga Sūtra and the practical technologies of consciousness to enliven this knowledge in everyone.

Contents

Samādhi-Pāda

Chapter on Transcendence

अथ योगानुशासनम् ।।१।।

atha yogānuśāsanam

atha now *yoga* union, integration *anuśāsanam* teaching, exposition

Now is the teaching on Yoga. (1)

योगश्चित्तवृत्तिनिरोधः ।।२।।

yogaś citta-vṛtti-nirodhaḥ

yogaḥ union, transcendental consciousness *citta* mind *vṛtti* activity *nirodhaḥ* complete settling, cessation

Yoga is the complete settling of the activity of the mind. (2)

तदा द्रष्टुः स्वरूपेऽवस्थानम् ।।३।।

tadā draṣṭuḥ svarūpe 'vasthānam

tadā then *draṣṭuḥ* of the observer *svarūpe* in own form, in own nature, in himself *avasthānam* establishment

Then the observer is established in the Self. (3)

वृत्तिसारूप्यमितरत्र ।।४।।

vṛtti-sārūpyam itaratra

vṛtti activity, impulse, tendency, reverberation *sārūpyam* same form, identification, emergence *itaḥ* from here *atra* here (*itaratra* is usually translated as "elsewhere.")

Reverberations of the Self emerge from here
(the self-referral state) and remain here
(within the self-referral state). (4)

वृत्तयः पञ्चतय्यः क्लिष्टाक्लिष्टाः ।।५।।

vṛttayaḥ pañcatayyaḥ kliṣṭākliṣṭāḥ

vṛttayaḥ activities *pañcatayyaḥ* fivefold *kliṣṭa* painful, suffering *akliṣṭāḥ* not painful, free from suffering

Mental activities are fivefold: painful and not painful. (5)

प्रमाणविपर्ययविकल्पनिद्रास्मृतयः ।।६।।

pramāṇa-viparyaya-vikalpa-nidrā-smṛtayaḥ

pramāṇa valid knowledge *viparyaya* invalid knowledge, misconception *vikalpa* imagination *nidrā* sleep *smṛtayaḥ* memory

They are valid knowledge, invalid knowledge, imagination, sleep and memory. (6)

प्रत्यक्षानुमानागमाः प्रमाणानि ॥७॥

pratyakṣānumānāgamāḥ pramāṇāni

pratyakṣa perception, direct experience *anumāna* inference *āgamāḥ* verbal testimony *pramāṇāni* valid knowledge

The means of gaining valid knowledge are direct experience, inference and verbal testimony. (7)

विपर्ययो मिथ्याज्ञानमतद्रूपप्रतिष्ठम् ॥८॥

viparyayo mithyā-jñānam atad-rūpa-pratiṣṭham

viparyayaḥ invalid knowledge *mithyā* deceptive, false *jñānam* understanding, knowledge *atat* not that (not real) *rūpa* form, appearance *pratiṣṭham* base, foundation

Invalid knowledge is deceptive understanding, based upon an appearance which is not real. (8)

शब्दज्ञानानुपाती वस्तुशून्यो विकल्पः ॥९॥

śabda-jñānānupātīvastu-śūnyo vikalpaḥ

śabda name, verbal *jñāna* knowledge *anupātī* follows, dependent upon *vastu* object *śūnyaḥ* devoid, without *vikalpaḥ* imagination

Imagination follows verbal knowledge, but without a corresponding object. (9)

अभावप्रत्ययालम्बना वृत्तिर्निद्रा ॥१०॥

abhāva-pratyayālambanā vṛttir nidrā

abhāva non-existence *pratyaya* experience *ālambanā* base, foundation *vṛttiḥ* state, activity *nidrā* sleep

Sleep is activity based in the experience of nonexistence. (10)

अनुभूतविषयासंप्रमोषः स्मृतिः ।।११।।

anubhūta-viṣayāsaṃpramoṣaḥ smṛtiḥ

anubhūta perceived *viṣaya* object *asaṃpramoṣaḥ* nonslipping away *smṛtiḥ* memory

Memory is not forgetting a perceived object. (11)

अभ्यासवैराग्याभ्यां तन्निरोधः ।।१२।।

abhyāsa-vairāgyābhyāṃ tan-nirodhaḥ

abhyāsa practice *vairāgyābhyām* through non-attachment *tat* these (activities) *nirodhaḥ* cessation, stilled

Through practice and non-attachment, these activities are stilled. (12)

तत्र स्थितौ यत्नोऽभ्यासः ।।१३।।

tatra sthitau yatno 'bhyāsaḥ

tatra there, in that (state of yoga) *sthitau* in the establishment *yatnaḥ* endeavor *abhyāsaḥ* practice

Practice is the endeavor to become established in the state of yoga. (13)

स तु दीर्घकालनैरन्तर्यसत्कारासेवितो दृढभूमिः ।।१४।।

sa tu dīrgha-kāla-nairantarya-satkārāsevitodṛḍha-bhūmiḥ

saḥ that (yoga) *tu* but, then *dīrgha* long *kāla* time *nairantarya* uninterrupted, without interval *satkāra* respectful *āsevitaḥ* cultivated, practiced *dṛḍha* firm *bhūmiḥ* established, grounded

Yoga becomes firmly established through regular and respectful practice for a long time. (14)

दृष्टानुश्रविकविषयवितृष्णस्य वशीकार संज्ञा वैराग्यम् ।।१५।।

dṛṣṭānuśravika-viṣaya-vitṛṣṇasya vaśīkāra-saṃjñā vairāgyam

dṛṣṭa seen *anuśravika* heard *viṣaya* object *vitṛṣṇasya* of one who has freedom from thirst or desire *vaśīkāra* mastery, triumph (of the Self) *saṃjñā* knowledge, indication, sign *vairāgyam* state of non-attachment

In the state of non-attachment one is freed from desire for objects, whether seen or heard of. This is the indication of the triumph of the Self. (15)

तत्परं पुरुषख्यातेर्गुणवैतृष्णयम् ।।१६।।

tat-paraṃ puruṣa-khyāter guṇa-vaitṛṣṇyam

tat that (state of non-attachment) *param* highest *puruṣa* Self, consciousness *khyāteḥ* through knowledge *guṇa* quality, change *vairṣṇyam* freedom

The highest state of non-attachment is freedom from all change, which comes through knowledge of the Self (*puruṣa*). (16)

वितर्कविचारानन्दास्मितारूपानुगमात्
संप्रज्ञातः ॥१७॥

vitarka-vicārānandāsmitā-rūpānugamāt saṃprajñātaḥ

vitarka gross mental activity, discursive thought *vicāra* subtle mental activity *ānanda* bliss *asmitā* pure individuality, "amness" *rūpa* form *anugamāt* through movement, through following *saṃprajñātaḥ* transcending with an object of attention

Samādhi with an object of attention (*saṃprajñātaḥ samādhi*) takes the form of gross mental activity, then subtle mental activity, bliss and the state of amness. (17)

विरामप्रत्ययाभ्यासपूर्वः
संस्कारशेषोऽन्यः ॥१८॥

virāma-pratyayābhyāsa-pūrvaḥ saṃskāra-śeṣo 'nyaḥ

virāma cessation *pratyaya* experience *abhyāsa* practice, repeated experience *pūrvaḥ* previous, preceded by, follows *saṃskāra* latent impression *śeṣaḥ* remain *anyaḥ* the other (state)

The other state, *samādhi* without an object of attention (*asaṃprajñātaḥ samādhi*), follows the repeated experience of cessation, although latent impressions still remain. (18)

भवप्रत्ययो विदेहप्रकृतिलयानाम् ॥१९॥

bhava-pratyayo videha-prakṛti-layānām

bhava being, becoming *pratyayaḥ* experience (*bhava-pratyayaḥ* experience of being, birth) *videha* one who lives at refined levels *prakṛti* nature *layānām* merged

By virtue of birth, some may live at refined levels or become merged with nature. (19)

श्रद्धावीर्यस्मृतिसमाधिप्रज्ञापूर्वक
इतरेषाम् ।।२०।।

śraddhā-vīrya-smṛti-samādhi-prajñā-pūrvaka itareṣām

śraddhā faith *vīrya* vigor *smṛti* memory *samādhi* transcendence *prajñā* knowledge *pūrvakaḥ* preceded by *itareṣām* for others

For others it is preceded by faith, vigor, memory, transcendence and knowledge. (20)

तीव्रसंवेगानामासन्नः ।।२१।।

tīvra-saṃvegānām āsannaḥ

tīvra strong, ardent *saṃvegānām* for those who are intent *āsannaḥ* near

It is near for those who are highly intent. (21)

मृदुमध्याधिमात्रत्वात्ततोऽपि विशेषः ॥२२॥

mṛdu-madhyādhimātratvāt tato 'pi viśeṣaḥ

mṛdu mild *madhya* middle, moderate *adhimātratvāt* from being very strong, above measure *tataḥ* from those *api* even *viśeṣaḥ* distinction, difference

Even among those, there is a distinction between mild, moderate and very strong. (22)

ईश्वरप्रणिधानाद्वा ॥२३॥

īśvara-praṇidhānād vā

īśvara God *praṇidhānāt* through devotion *vā* or

Or it is obtained through devotion to God. (23)

क्लेशकर्मविपाकाशयैरपरामृष्टः पुरुषविशेष ईश्वरः ॥२४॥

kleśa-karma-vipākāśayair aparāmṛṣṭaḥ puruṣaviśeṣa īśvaraḥ

kleśa affliction, suffering *karma* action *vipāka* ripening, fruit (of action) *āśayaiḥ* by impressions *aparāmṛṣṭaḥ* unaffected, untouched *puruṣa* being, person, personality *viśeṣa* distinct, particular *īśvaraḥ* God

God is a distinct personality, unaffected by afflictions, action, the result of action, or impressions. (24)

तत्र निरतिशयं सर्वज्ञबीजम् ॥२५॥

tatra niratiśayaṃ sarvajña-bījam

tatra there, in Him *niratiśayam* unsurpassed *sarvajña* omniscience *bījam* seed

In Him the seed of omniscience is unsurpassed. (25)

स पूर्वेषामपि गुरुः
कालेनानवच्छेदात् ।।२६।।

sa pūrveṣām api guruḥ kālenānavacchedāt

saḥ He *pūrveṣām* of the former, of the ancients *api* also *guruḥ* teacher *kālena* by time *anavacchedāt* from not being bound

He is also the teacher of the ancients, being unbound by time. (26)

तस्य वाचकः प्रणवः ।।२७।।

tasya vācakaḥ praṇavaḥ

tasya of Him *vācakaḥ* expression *praṇavaḥ* sound

The expression of Him is sound. (27)

तज्जपस्तदर्थभावनम् ॥२८॥

taj-japas tad-artha-bhāvanam

tat that *japaḥ* repeated experience, repetition *tat* that *artha* form, meaning *bhāvanam* production, creation

Repeated experience of that produces the form of that. (28)

ततः प्रत्यक्चेतनाधिगमोऽप्यन्तरायाभावश्च ॥२९॥

tataḥ pratyak-cetanādhigamo 'py antarāyābhāvaś ca

tataḥ then *pratyak* inward *cetanā* awareness *adhigamaḥ* going *api* also, as well *antarāya* obstacles *abhāvaḥ* disappearance *ca* and

Then the awareness turns inward, and obstacles disappear as well. (29)

व्याधिस्त्यानसंशयप्रमादालस्याविरति-
भ्रान्तिदर्शनालब्धभूमिकत्वानवस्थितत्वानि
चित्तविक्षेपास्तेऽन्तरायाः ॥३०॥

vyādhi-styāna-saṃśaya-pramādālasyāviratibhrānti-
darśanālabdha-bhūmikatvānavasthitatvāni
citta-vikṣepās te 'ntarāyāḥ

vyādhi disease *styāna* fatigue *saṃśaya* doubt *pramāda* carelessness *ālasya* laziness *avirati* attachment *bhrānti* confused *darśana* vision, understanding (*bhrānti-darśana* delusion) *alabdha* unobtained *bhūmikatva* stage (*alabdha-bhūmikatva* failure to achieve the stages) *anavasthitatvāni* instability *citta* mind *vikṣepāḥ* distractions *te* those *antarāyāḥ* obstacles

Those obstacles that distract the mind are disease, fatigue, doubt, carelessness, laziness, attachment, confused understanding, failure to achieve *samādhi* and failure to maintain *samādhi*. (30)

दुःखदौर्मनस्याङ्गमेजयत्वश्वासप्रश्वासा
विक्षेपसहभुवः ।।३१।।

*duḥkha-daurmanasyāṅgam-ejayatva-śvāsa-
praśvāsā vikṣepa-sahabhuvaḥ*

duḥkha pain *daurmanasya* depression *aṅgam* limb *ejayatva* shaking *śvāsa* inhalation *praśvāsāḥ* exhalation *vikṣepa* distraction *sahabhuvaḥ* accompanying

These distractions are accompanied by pain, depression, restlessness and coarse breathing. (31)

तत्प्रतिषेधार्थमेकतत्त्वाभ्यासः ।।३२।।

tat-pratiṣedhārtham eka-tattvābhyāsaḥ

tat these (obstacles) *pratiṣedha* removal, prevention *artham* goal, purpose *eka* one, single *tattva* reality, principle *abhyāsaḥ* practice, repeated experience

These obstacles can be removed by repeated experience of the one reality. (32)

मैत्रीकरुणामुदितोपेक्षाणां
सुखदुःखपुण्यापुण्यविषयाणां
भावनातश्चित्तप्रसादनम् ।।३३।।

maitrī-karuṇā-muditopekṣāṇāṃ
sukha-duḥkha-puṇyāpuṇya-viṣayāṇāṃ
bhāvanātaś citta-prasādanam

maitrī friendliness *karuṇā* compassion *muditā* delight, happiness, joy *upekṣāṇām* for those having equanimity *sukha* happy *duḥkha* unhappy *puṇya* virtuous *apuṇya* unvirtuous *viṣayāṇām* for those having spheres of activity *bhāvanātaḥ* by cultivating *citta* mind *prasādanam* purification

The mind becomes purified by cultivating friendliness toward the happy, compassion toward the unhappy, delight in the virtuous and equanimity toward the unvirtuous. (33)

प्रच्छर्दनविधारणाभ्यां वा प्राणस्य ।।३४।।

pracchardana-vidhāraṇābhyāṃ vā prāṇasya

pracchardana exhalation *vidhāraṇābhyām* by inhalation *vā* or *prāṇasya* of the breath

Or the mind becomes purified by inhalation and exhalation of the breath. (34)

विषयवती वा प्रवृत्तिरुत्पन्ना मनसः स्थितिनिबन्धनी ।।३५।।

viṣayavatī vā pravṛttir utpannā manasaḥ sthiti-nibandhanī

viṣayavatī having object (of refined perception) *vā* or *pravṛttiḥ* cognition *utpannā* arising *manasaḥ* of mind *sthiti* steadiness *nibandhanī* established

Or steadiness of mind is established when the cognition of refined perception arises. (35)

विशोका वा ज्योतिष्मती ॥३६॥

viśokā vā jyotiṣmatī

viśokā free from sorrow *vā* or *jyotiṣmatī* light filled

Or by the experience of inner light, which is free from sorrow. (36)

वीतरागविषयं वा चित्तम् ॥३७॥

vīta-rāga-viṣayaṃ vā cittam

vīta free from *rāga* desire, passion *viṣayam* object, condition *vā* or *cittam* mind

Or by attuning the mind to a person free from desire. (37)

स्वप्ननिद्राज्ञानालम्बनं वा ॥३८॥

svapna-nidrā-jñānālambanaṃ vā

svapna dreaming *nidrā* deep sleep *jñāna* knowledge *ālambanam* obtaining, resting upon *vā* or

Or by knowledge obtained in dreaming or deep sleep. (38)

यथाभिमतध्यानाद्वा ॥३९॥

yathābhimata-dhyānād vā

yathā as, accordingly *abhimata* desired, pleasing, agreeable *dhyānāt* from meditation *vā* or

Or from meditation on what is agreeable. (39)

परमाणुपरममहत्त्वान्तोऽस्य
वशीकारः ॥४०॥

paramāṇu-parama-mahattvānto 'sya vaśīkāraḥ

parama extreme, supremely *aṇu* small *parama* extreme, supremely *mahattva* great *antaḥ* end *asya* of this *vaśīkāraḥ* mastery

Mastery of this extends from the smallest of the small to the greatest of the great. (40)

क्षीणवृत्तेरभिजातस्येव मणेर्ग्रहीतृग्रहणग्राह्येषु
तत्स्थतदञ्जनता समापत्तिः ।।४१।।

kṣīṇa-vṛtter abhijātasyeva maṇer grahītṛ-grahaṇa-grāhyeṣu tat-stha-tad-añjanatā samāpattiḥ

kṣīṇa diminished, decreased *vṛtteḥ* of the activity *abhijātasya* of a transparent, of a well-polished *iva* like *maṇeḥ* of a crystal *grahītṛ* knower, grasper *grahaṇa* knowing, grasping *grāhyeṣu* in the known, in the grasped *tat* that *stha* resting, standing *tat* that *añjanatā* appearance *samāpattiḥ* absorption

When mental activity decreases, then knower, knowing and known become absorbed one into another, like a transparent crystal which assumes the appearance of that upon which it rests. (41)

तत्र शब्दार्थज्ञानविकल्पैः संकीर्णा सवितर्का समापत्तिः ।।४२।।

tatra śabdārtha-jñāna-vikalpaiḥ saṃkīrṇā savitarkā samāpattiḥ

tatra there (in the first stage of absorption, *savitarkā*) *śabda* sound *artha* object, meaning *jñāna* idea *vikalpaiḥ* by alternating *saṃkīrṇā* mixed, disordered, unresolved *savitarkā* with deliberation, with reasoning *samāpattiḥ* absorption

In the first stage of absorption (*savitarkā samāpatti*) the mind is mixed—alternating between sound, object and idea. (42)

स्मृतिपरिशुद्धौ स्वरूपशून्येवार्थमात्र-
निर्भासा निर्वितर्का ॥४३॥

*smṛti-pariśuddhau svarūpa-śūnyevārtha-mātra-
nirbhāsā nirvitarkā*

smṛti memory *pariśuddhau* in the clarification, in the purification *svarūpa* own nature *śūnyā* devoid *iva* as it were *artha* gross object *mātra* only *nirbhāsā* appearance *nirvitarkā* without deliberation

In the second stage of absorption (*nirvitarkā*) the memory is clarified, yet devoid of its own nature, as it were, and only the gross object appears. (43)

एतयैव सविचारा निर्विचारा च
सूक्ष्मविषया व्याख्याता ॥४४॥

etayaiva savicāra nirvicāra ca sūkṣma-viṣayā vyākhyātā

etayā by this *eva* thus *savicāra* with reflection *nirvicāra* without reflection *ca* and *sūkṣma* subtle *viṣayā* object *vyākhyātā* explained

The third stage (*savicāra*) and fourth stage (*nirvicāra*) are explained in the same way, only with a subtle object of attention. (44)

सूक्ष्मविषयत्वं चालिङ्गपर्यवसानम् ॥४५॥

sūkṣma-viṣayatvaṃ cāliṅga-paryavasānam

sūkṣma subtle *viṣayatvam* objectness *ca* and *aliṅga* formless *paryavasānam* end, extent

And the range of subtle objects extends to the formless. (45)

ता एव सबीजः समाधिः ॥४६॥

tā eva sabījaḥ samādhiḥ

tāḥ these *eva* still *sabījaḥ* with object, with seed *samādhiḥ* transcending

These levels of *samādhi* still have objects of attention. (46)

निर्विचारवैशारद्येऽध्यात्मप्रसादः ॥४७॥

nirvicāra-vaiśāradye 'dhyātma-prasādaḥ

nirvicāra without reflection *vaiśāradye* in the clear experience, in the expertness *adhyātma* regarding the Self, spiritual *prasādaḥ* brightness, splendor, clarity, tranquility

In the clear experience of *nirvicāra samādhi* dawns the splendor of spirituality. (47)

ऋतम्भरा तत्र प्रज्ञा ॥४८॥

ṛtambharā tatra prajñā

ṛtambharā truth bearing *tatra* there *prajñā* intellect

There resides the intellect that knows only the truth. (48)

श्रुतानुमानप्रज्ञाभ्यामन्यविषया विशेषार्थत्वात् ॥४९॥

śrutānumāna-prajñābhyām anya-viṣayā viśeṣārthatvāt

śruta verbal testimony *anumāna* inference *prajñābhyām* than knowledge *anya* other, different *viṣayā* object, range of knowledge *viśeṣa* specific *arthatvāt* from the object

Because it is directed toward a specific object, the range of knowledge obtained in *ṛtambharā prajñā* is different from knowledge obtained through verbal testimony or inference. (49)

तज्जः संस्कारोऽन्यसंस्कारप्रतिबन्धी ॥५०॥

taj-jaḥ saṃskāro 'nya-saṃskāra-pratibandhī

tat that (state) *jaḥ* arising *saṃskāraḥ* impression *anya* other *saṃskāra* impression *pratibandhī* preventing, excluding

The impression arising from that state prevents other impressions. (50)

तस्यापि निरोधे सर्वनिरोधान्निर्बीजः समाधिः ।।५१।।

tasyāpi nirodhe sarva-nirodhān nirbījaḥ samādhiḥ

tasya of that (state) *api* also *nirodhe* in the settling *sarva* all *nirodhāt* from the calming *nirbījaḥ* without seed, unbounded *samādhiḥ* wakefulness, transcendence

In the settling of that state also, all is calmed, and what remains is unbounded wakefulness. (51)

Sādhana-Pāda

Chapter on Practice

तपःस्वाध्यायेश्वरप्रणिधानानि
क्रियायोगः ॥१॥

tapaḥ-svādhyāyeśvara-praṇidhānāni kriyā-yogaḥ

tapaḥ abstainment *svādhyāya* study of the Self *īśvara* God *praṇidhānāni* devotion *kriyā* activity *yogaḥ* union, integration

Tapas, study of the Self and devotion to God constitute the yoga of activity. (1)

समाधिभावनार्थः क्लेशतनूकरणार्थश्च ॥२॥

samādhi-bhāvanārthaḥ kleśa-tanū-karaṇārthaś ca

samādhi even intellect, transcendental consciousness *bhāvana* cultivation *arthaḥ* purpose *kleśa* affliction, cause of suffering *tanū* weak *karaṇa* making *arthaḥ* purpose *ca* and

The purpose of the yoga of activity is to cultivate *samādhi* and to weaken afflictions, the causes of suffering. (2)

अविद्यास्मितारागद्वेषाभिनिवेशाः क्लेशाः ।।३।।

avidyāsmitā-rāga-dveṣābhiniveśāḥ kleśāḥ

avidyā ignorance *asmitā* individuality *rāga* attachment *dveṣa* aversion *abhiniveśāḥ* clinging to life *kleśāḥ* afflictions, causes of suffering

The causes of suffering are ignorance, individuality, attachment, aversion and clinging to life. (3)

अविद्या क्षेत्रमुत्तरेषां प्रसुप्ततनुविच्छिन्नोदाराणाम् ।।४।।

avidyā kṣetram uttareṣāṃ prasupta-tanu-vicchinnodārāṇām

avidyā ignorance *kṣetram* field, source *uttareṣām* of the others *prasupta* dormant *tanu* weak *vicchinna* suspended *udārāṇām* of the active

Ignorance is the source of the others, whether they are dormant, weak, suspended or active. (4)

अनित्याशुचिदुःखानात्मसु नित्यशुचिसुखात्मख्यातिरविद्या ॥५॥

anityāśuci-duḥkhānātmasu nitya-śuci-sukhātma-khyātir avidyā

anitya non-eternal *aśuci* impure *duḥkha* suffering *anātmasu* in the non-Self *nitya* eternal *śuci* pure *sukha* happiness *ātma* Self *khyātiḥ* perceiving *avidyā* ignorance

Ignorance is perceiving the non-eternal as eternal, the impure as pure, suffering as happiness, and the non-Self as Self. (5)

दृग्दर्शनशक्त्योरेकात्मतेवास्मिता ॥६॥

dṛg-darśana-śaktyor ekātmatevāsmitā

dṛg seer *darśana* seen *śaktyoḥ* of the capacities, of the capabilities *eka* one *ātmatā* nature (*ekātmatā* identification) *iva* as it were *asmitā* individuality

Individuality is identifying, as it were, the capacity of seer and seen. (6)

सुखानुशयी रागः ॥७॥

sukhānuśayī rāgaḥ

sukha pleasure *anuśayī* following, result of *rāgaḥ* attachment

Attachment is the result of pleasure. (7)

दुःखानुशयी द्वेषः ॥८॥

duḥkhānuśayī dveṣaḥ

duḥkha pain *anuśayī* following, result of *dveṣaḥ* aversion

Aversion is the result of pain. (8)

स्वरसवाही विदुषोऽपि तथा
रूढोऽभिनिवेशः ।।९।।

svarasa-vāhī viduṣo 'pi tathā rūḍho 'bhiniveśaḥ

svarasa own essence *vāhī* flowing *viduṣaḥ* learned, wise *api* even *tathā* thus *rūḍhaḥ* arising *abhiniveśaḥ* clinging to life

Clinging to life is spontaneous, thus arising even in the learned. (9)

ते प्रतिप्रसवहेयाः सूक्ष्माः ।।१०।।

te pratiprasava-heyāḥ sūkṣmāḥ

te these (afflictions) *pratiprasava* returning to original state *heyāḥ* to be removed, to be averted *sūkṣmāḥ* subtle

These afflictions, when subtle, are removed by returning to one's original state. (10)

ध्यानहेयास्तद्वृत्तयः ।।११।।

dhyāna-heyās tad-vṛttayaḥ

dhyāna meditation *heyāḥ* to be removed *tat* they
vṛttayaḥ active, excited

When active, they are removed by meditation. (11)

क्लेशमूलः कर्माशयो
दृष्टादृष्टजन्मवेदनीयः ।।१२।।

kleśa-mūlaḥ karmāśayo dṛṣṭādṛṣṭa-janma-vedanīyaḥ

kleśa affliction *mūlaḥ* root *karma* (past) action *āśayaḥ* storehouse
dṛṣṭa seen, present *adṛṣṭa* unseen, future *janma* birth, life *vedanīyaḥ*
to be expressed, to be known

Afflictions are at the root of the storehouse of past action,
which becomes expressed in the present or future life. (12)

सति मूले तद्विपाको जात्यायुर्भोगाः ।।१३।।

sati mūle tad-vipāko jāty-āyur-bhogāḥ

sati existing *mūle* in the root *tat* that (storehouse of past action) *vipākaḥ* fruition *jāti* birth *āyuḥ* life span *bhogāḥ* experiences

As long as its root exists, the storehouse of past action will generate more births, more life spans, more experiences. (13)

ते ह्लादपरितापफलाः
पुण्यापुण्यहेतुत्वात् ।।१४।।

te hlāda-paritāpa-phalāḥ puṇyāpuṇya-hetutvāt

te these (births, life spans, experiences) *hlāda* pleasure *paritāpa* pain *phalāḥ* fruits *puṇya* virtuous *apuṇya* unvirtuous *hetutvāt* from the cause

If these births are caused by virtuous action, they are pleasurable. If caused by unvirtuous action, they are painful. (14)

परिणामतापसंस्कारदुःखैर्गुणवृत्तिविरोधाच्च दुःखमेव सर्वं विवेकिनः ।।१५।।

pariṇāma-tāpa-saṃskāra-duḥkhair guṇa-vṛttivirodhāc ca duḥkham eva sarvaṃ vivekinaḥ

pariṇāma transformation, change *tāpa* anxiety *saṃskāra* impression *duḥkhaiḥ* by suffering *guṇa* nature, quality *vṛtti* activity *virodhāt* from opposing, from contradicting *ca* and *duḥkham* suffering *eva* indeed *sarvam* all, everyone *vivekinaḥ* discriminating persons

Suffering is caused by change, anxiety, impressions, and by opposing the activity of nature. Indeed, discriminating persons know that everyone is suffering. (15)

हेयं दुःखमनागतम् ।।१६।।

heyaṃ duḥkham anāgatam

heyam to be averted, to be abandoned *duḥkham* suffering, danger *anāgatam* not yet come

Avert the danger which has not yet come. (16)

द्रष्टृदृश्ययोः संयोगो हेयहेतुः ।।१७।।

draṣṭṛ-dṛśyayoḥ saṃyogo heya-hetuḥ

draṣṭṛ seer *dṛśyayoḥ* of the seen *saṃyogaḥ* identification
heya to be averted *hetuḥ* cause (of the danger)

The cause of the danger to be averted is the identification of seer and seen. (17)

प्रकाशक्रियास्थितिशीलं भूतेन्द्रियात्मकं
भोगापवर्गार्थं दृश्यम् ।।१८।।

prakāśa-kriyā-sthiti-śīlaṃ bhūtendriyātmakaṃ
bhogāpavargārthaṃ dṛśyam

prakāśa luminosity *kriyā* activity *sthiti* inertia *śīlam* quality *bhūta* element *indriya* sense *ātmakam* consisting of *bhoga* experience *apavarga* liberation *artham* purpose *dṛśyam* seen

The seen—consisting of the elements and senses—has the qualities of luminosity, activity and inertia. Its purpose is to provide experience leading to liberation. (18)

विशेषाविशेषलिङ्गमात्रालिङ्गानि
गुणपर्वाणि ॥१९॥

viśeṣāviśeṣa-liṅga-mātrāliṅgāni guṇa-parvāṇi

viśeṣa distinct (*mahābhūtas, karmendriyas, jñānendriyas, manas*) *aviśeṣa* indistinct (*tanmātras, ahaṃkāra*) *liṅga* with mark (*buddhi*) *mātra* only *aliṅgāni* without marks (*prakṛti*) *guṇa* quality, nature *parvāṇi* divisions

The divisions of the *guṇas* are distinct, indistinct, with mark only and without marks. (19)

द्रष्टा दृशिमात्रः शुद्धोऽपि
प्रत्ययानुपश्यः ॥२०॥

draṣṭā dṛśi-mātraḥ śuddho 'pi pratyayānupaśyaḥ

draṣṭā seer *dṛśi* perceiver *mātraḥ* only *śuddhaḥ* pure *api* although *pratyaya* intelligence (*buddhi*) *anupaśyaḥ* reflected, perceived

The seer is a perceiver only. Although pure, it is perceived through intelligence. (20)

तदर्थ एव दृश्यस्यात्मा ।।२१।।

tad-artha eva dṛśyasyātmā

tat that (seer) *arthaḥ* purpose *eva* solely *dṛśyasya* of the seen *ātmā* existence

The existence of the seen is solely to fulfill the purpose of the seer. (21)

कृतार्थं प्रति नष्टमप्यनष्टं तदन्यसाधारणत्वात् ।।२२।।

kṛtārthaṃ prati naṣṭam apy anaṣṭaṃ tad-anya-sādhāraṇatvāt

kṛta done, accomplished *artham* purpose *prati* for *naṣṭam* destroyed, disappeared *api* still *anaṣṭam* not destroyed *tat* it (seen) *anya* other *sādhāraṇatvāt* because of commonality

Although the seen has disappeared for one whose purpose is accomplished, still it is not destroyed because it is common to others. (22)

स्वस्वामिशक्त्योः स्वरूपोपलब्धिहेतुः संयोगः ।।२३।।

sva-svāmi-śaktyoḥ svarūpopalabdhi-hetuḥ saṃyogaḥ

sva owned, seen *svāmi* owner, seer *śaktyoḥ* of the capacities *svarūpa* own form, essential nature *upalabdhi* obtained, known *hetuḥ* cause *saṃyogaḥ* identification

The seer is identified with the seen so that the essential nature of each may be known. (23)

तस्य हेतुरविद्या ।।२४।।

tasya hetur avidyā

tasya of that (identification) *hetuḥ* cause *avidyā* ignorance

The cause of identification is ignorance. (24)

तदभावात्संयोगाभावो हानं तद्दृशेः
कैवल्यम् ।।२५।।

tad-abhāvāt saṃyogābhāvo hānaṃ tad dṛśeḥ kaivalyam

tat that (ignorance) *abhāvāt* from the elimination *saṃyoga* identification *abhāvaḥ* elimination *hānam* release *tat* that *dṛśeḥ* of seeing, of awareness *kaivalyam* singularity, enlightenment

Eliminating ignorance eliminates identification.
That is release—singularity of awareness, *kaivalya*. (25)

विवेकख्यातिरविप्लवा हानोपायः ।२६।।

viveka-khyātir aviplavā hānopāyaḥ

viveka discrimination *khyātiḥ* knowledge, vision *aviplavā* undisturbed *hāna* release *upāyaḥ* means

The means of release is undisturbed discriminative knowledge. (26)

तस्य सप्तधा प्रान्तभूमिः प्रज्ञा ।।२७।।

tasya saptadhā prānta-bhūmiḥ prajñā

tasya for that *saptadhā* seven *prānta* culminating, last *bhūmiḥ* level, stage *prajñā* wisdom, complete wakefulness

For that, there are seven stages, culminating in complete wakefulness. (27)

योगाङ्गानुष्ठानादशुद्धिक्षये
ज्ञानदीप्तिराविवेकख्यातेः ।।२८।।

yogāṅgānuṣṭhānād aśuddhi-kṣaye jñāna-dīptir ā viveka-khyāteḥ

yoga union, integration *aṅga* limb *anuṣṭhānāt* through the practice, through the exercise *aśuddhi* impurity *kṣaye* in the destruction *jñāna* knowledge *dīptiḥ* light *ā* up to *viveka* discrimination *khyāteḥ* of knowledge, of awareness

When impurity is destroyed through the practice of the limbs of yoga, then the light of knowledge leads to discriminative awareness. (28)

यमनियमासनप्राणायामप्रत्याहारधारणा-
ध्यानसमाधयोऽष्टावङ्गानि ॥२९॥

yama-niyamāsana-prāṇāyāma-pratyāhāradhāraṇā-dhyāna-samādhayo 'ṣṭāv aṅgāni

yama observance *niyama* rule *āsana* posture *prāṇāyāma* regulation of breathing *pratyāhāra* retirement *dhāraṇā* steadiness *dhyāna* meditation *samādhayaḥ* even intellect, transcendental consciousness *aṣṭau* eight *aṅgāni* limbs

The eight limbs are observance (*yama*), rule (*niyama*), posture (*āsana*), regulation of breathing (*prāṇāyāma*), retirement (*pratyāhāra*), steadiness (*dhāraṇā*), meditation (*dhyāna*) and transcendental consciousness (*samādhi*). (29)

अहिंसासत्यास्तेयब्रह्मचर्यापरिग्रहा
यमाः ॥३०॥

ahiṃsā-satyāsteya-brahmacaryāparigrahā yamāḥ

ahiṃsā non-injury *satya* truthfulness *asteya* non-theft *brahmacarya* celibacy *aparigrahāḥ* non-possession *yamāḥ* observances

The *yamas* are non-injury (*ahiṃsā*), truthfulness (*satya*), non-theft (*asteya*), celibacy (*brahmacarya*) and non-possession (*aparigraha*). (30)

जातिदेशकालसमयानवच्छिन्नाः
सार्वभौमा महाव्रतम् ॥३१॥

jāti-deśa-kāla-samayānavacchinnāḥ
sārva-bhaumā mahā-vratam

jāti birth *deśa* place *kāla* time *samaya* circumstance *anavacchinnāḥ* unqualified by *sārva* all *bhaumāḥ* levels (*sārva-bhaumāḥ* universal) *mahā* great *vratam* resolve, law

These great laws are universal—not qualified by birth, place, time or circumstance. (31)

शौचसंतोषतपःस्वाध्यायेश्वरप्रणिधानानि नियमाः ॥३२॥

śauca-saṃtoṣa-tapaḥ-svādhyāyeśvara-praṇidhānāni niyamāḥ

śauca purification *saṃtoṣa* contentment *tapaḥ* abstainment, increasing glow *svādhyāya* self-study *īśvara* God *praṇidhānāni* devotion *niyamāḥ* rules

The *niyamas* are purification (*śauca*), contentment (*saṃtoṣa*), abstainment (*tapas*), study of the Self (*svādhyāya*) and devotion to God (*īśvara-praṇidhāna*). (32)

वितर्कबाधने प्रतिपक्षभावनम् ॥३३॥

vitarka-bādhane pratipakṣa-bhāvanam

vitarka negativity *bādhane* in removing *pratipakṣa* opposite *bhāvanam* cultivating, producing

For removing negativity, the opposite should be cultivated. (33)

वितर्का हिंसादयः कृतकारितानुमोदिता लोभक्रोधमोहपूर्वका मृदुमध्याधिमात्रा दुःखाज्ञानानन्तफला इति प्रतिपक्षभावनम् ।।३४।।

vitarkā hiṃsādayaḥ kṛta-kāritānumoditā lobha-krodha-moha-pūrvakā mṛdu-madhyādhimātrā duḥkhājñānānanta-phalā iti pratipakṣa-bhāvanam

vitarkāḥ negativity *hiṃsā* injury *ādayaḥ* and so on *kṛta* done *kārita* caused to be done *anumoditāḥ* approved *lobha* greed *krodha* anger *moha* delusion *pūrvakāḥ* preceded *mṛdu* mild *madhya* moderate *adhimātrāḥ* intense *duḥkha* suffering *ajñāna* ignorance *ananta* unending *phalāḥ* fruits *iti* thus *pratipakṣa* opposite *bhāvanam* cultivating

Negativity, such as injury and so on—whether done directly, caused to be done, or approved of—is preceded by greed, anger and delusion. Whether mild, moderate or intense, its fruits are unending suffering and ignorance. Thus the opposite should be cultivated. (34)

अहिंसाप्रतिष्ठायां तत्सन्निधौ
वैरत्यागः ।।३५।।

ahiṃsā-pratiṣṭhāyāṃ tat-sannidhau vaira-tyāgaḥ

ahiṃsā non-injury *pratiṣṭhāyām* in establishing *tat* that *sannidhau* in the vicinity *vaira* enmity, hostile tendencies *tyāgaḥ* elimination, abandonment

Where non-injury is established, in the vicinity of that, hostile tendencies are eliminated. (35)

सत्यप्रतिष्ठायां क्रियाफलाश्रयत्वम् ।।३६।।

satya-pratiṣṭhāyāṃ kriyā-phalāśrayatvam

satya truthfulness *pratiṣṭhāyām* in establishing *kriyā* activity *phala* fruit *āśrayatvam* close connection, depending on

When truthfulness is established, activity and its fruit are closely connected. (36)

अस्तेयप्रतिष्ठायां सर्वरत्नोपस्थानम् ।।३७।।

asteya-pratiṣṭhāyāṃ sarva-ratnopasthānam

asteya non-theft *pratiṣṭhāyām* in establishing *sarva* all *ratna* jewel, wealth *upasthānam* rising up, approach, appearance

When non-theft is established, all jewels rise up. (37)

ब्रह्मचर्यप्रतिष्ठायां वीर्यलाभः ।।३८।।

brahmacarya-pratiṣṭhāyāṃ vīrya-lābhaḥ

brahmacarya celibacy *pratiṣṭhāyām* in establishing *vīrya* vigor, strength, vitality, luster *lābhaḥ* obtained

When celibacy is established, vitality is obtained. (38)

अपरिग्रहस्थैर्ये जन्मकथंतासंबोधः ।।३९।।

aparigraha-sthairye janma-kathaṃtā-saṃbodhaḥ

aparigraha non-possession *sthairye* in the steadfastness *janma* birth, existence *kathaṃtā* the how, the what *saṃbodhaḥ* knowledge

When non-possession is steadfast, knowledge comes regarding the questions of existence. (39)

शौचात्स्वाङ्गजुगुप्सा परैरसंसर्गः ।।४०।।

śaucāt svāṅga-jugupsā parair asaṃsargaḥ

śaucāt from purification *svāṅga* own limb, own body *jugupsā* desire to protect *paraiḥ* with others *asaṃsargaḥ* non-contact

From purification arises the desire to protect one's own body and freedom from contact with others. (40)

सत्त्वशुद्धिसौमनस्यैकाग्र्येन्द्रियजयात्म-
दर्शनयोग्यत्वानि च ।।४१।।

sattva-śuddhi-saumanasyaikāgryendriyajayātma-darśana-yogyatvāni ca

sattva intellect *śuddhi* purity, clarity *saumanasya* cheerfulness, gladness, satisfaction *eka* one *agrya* pointedness (*eka-agrya* one-pointedness, singleness of intent) *indriya* sense *jaya* mastery *ātma* Self *darśana* vision, realization *yogyatvāni* fitness *ca* and

Also come clarity of intellect, cheerfulness, onepointedness, mastery over the senses and fitness for Self-realization. (41)

संतोषादनुत्तमः सुखलाभः ।।४२।।

saṃtoṣād anuttamaḥ sukha-lābhaḥ

saṃtoṣāt from contentment *anuttamaḥ* unsurpassed *sukha* happiness *lābhaḥ* obtainment

From contentment, unsurpassed happiness is obtained. (42)

कायेन्द्रियसिद्धिरशुद्धिक्षयात्तपसः ।।४३।।

kāyendriya-siddhir aśuddhi-kṣayāt tapasaḥ

kāya body *indriya* sense *siddhiḥ* perfection *aśuddhi* impurity *kṣayāt* from destruction, from collapse *tapasaḥ* through abstainment, through increasing glow

From the destruction of impurity through *tapas,* there is perfection of the body and senses. (43)

स्वाध्यायादिष्टदेवतासंप्रयोगः ।।४४।।

svādhyāyād iṣṭa-devatā-saṃprayogaḥ

svādhyāyāt from self-study *iṣṭa* desired *devatā* impulse of nature *saṃprayogaḥ* union

From study of the Self there is union with the desired impulse of nature. (44)

समाधिसिद्धिरीश्वरप्रणिधानात् ।।४५।।

samādhi-siddhir īśvara-praṇidhānāt

samādhi even intellect, transcendental consciousness
siddhiḥ perfection *īśvara* God *praṇidhānāt* from devotion

From devotion to God, *samādhi* is perfected. (45)

स्थिरसुखमासनम् ।।४६।।

sthira-sukham āsanam

sthira steady *sukham* comfort, pleasantness *āsanam* posture

Āsana is steady pleasantness. (46)

प्रयत्नशैथिल्यानन्तसमापत्तिभ्याम् ।।४७।।

prayatna-śaithilyānanta-samāpattibhyām

prayatna effort, activity *śaithilya* relaxation *ananta* unboundedness, infinite *samāpattibhyām* by absorptions, by sequential steadiness

Āsana is perfected by relaxation of effort and the dawn of unboundedness. (47)

ततो द्वन्द्वानभिघातः ।।४८।।

tato dvandvānabhighātaḥ

tataḥ from that *dvandva* pairs of opposites (pleasure and pain, heat and cold, etc.) *anabhighātaḥ* non-disturbance, freedom

From that comes freedom from the pairs of opposites. (48)

तस्मिन्सति श्वासप्रश्वासयोर्गतिविच्छेदः
प्राणायामः ॥४९॥

tasmin sati śvāsa-praśvāsayor gati-vicchedaḥ prāṇāyāmaḥ

tasmin in that *sati* being *śvāsa* inhalation *praśvāsayoḥ* of exhalation *gati* movement *vicchedaḥ* suspension *prāṇāyāmaḥ* regulation of breathing

After accomplishing that, comes *prāṇāyāma*—the suspension of the movement of inhalation and exhalation. (49)

बाह्याभ्यन्तरस्तम्भवृत्तिर्देशकालसंख्याभिः
परिदृष्टो दीर्घसूक्ष्मः ॥५०॥

bāhyābhyantara-stambha-vṛttir deśa-kālasaṃkhyābhiḥ paridṛṣṭo dīrgha-sūkṣmaḥ

bāhya external *abhyantara* internal *stambha* completely suspended *vṛttiḥ* activity *deśa* place *kāla* time *saṃkhyābhiḥ* by number *paridṛṣṭaḥ* regulated *dīrgha* long *sūkṣmaḥ* subtle

The activity of breath may be external, internal or completely suspended. When regulated by place, time and number, the breath becomes long and subtle. (50)

बाह्याभ्यन्तरविषयाक्षेपी चतुर्थः ।।५१।।

bāhyābhyantara-viṣayākṣepī caturthaḥ

bāhya external *abhyantara* internal *viṣaya* object, domain *ākṣepī* going beyond *caturthaḥ* fourth

The fourth goes beyond the domain of external and internal. (51)

ततः क्षीयते प्रकाशावरणम् ।।५२।।

tataḥ kṣīyate prakāśāvaraṇam

tataḥ then *kṣīyate* is destroyed, is removed, is diminished *prakāśa* light *āvaraṇam* covering

Then the covering over the light is removed. (52)

धारणासु च योग्यता मनसः ।।५३।।

dhāraṇāsu ca yogyatā manasaḥ

dhāraṇāsu in steadiness *ca* and *yogyatā* fitness, ability *manasaḥ* of the mind

And the mind becomes fit for steadiness (*dhāraṇā*). (53)

स्वविषयासंप्रयोगे चित्तस्य स्वरूपानुकार इवेन्द्रियाणां प्रत्याहारः ।।५४।।

svaviṣayāsaṃprayoge cittasya svarūpānukāra ivendriyāṇāṃ pratyāhāraḥ

svaviṣaya own object *asaṃprayoge* in non-contact *cittasya* of the mind *svarūpa* essential nature *anukāra* following *iva* as it were *indriyāṇām* of the senses *pratyāhāraḥ* retirement (of the senses from their objects)

When there is no contact with their objects, the senses follow, as it were, the essential nature of the mind. This is retirement (*pratyāhāra*). (54)

ततः परमा वश्यतेन्द्रियाणाम् ।।५५।।

tataḥ paramā vaśyatendriyāṇām

tataḥ from that (*pratyāhāra*) *paramā* supreme, highest *vaśyatā* the state of being under control, mastery *indriyāṇām* of the senses

From *pratyāhāra*, mastery over the senses is supreme. (55)

Vibhūti-Pāda

Chapter on Special Abilities

देशबन्धश्चित्तस्य धारणा ।।१।।

deśa-bandhaś cittasya dhāraṇā

deśa place, point *bandhaḥ* fixity, focus, held steady *cittasya* of mind, of attention *dhāraṇā* steadiness

Dhāraṇā is attention held steady on a single point. (1)

तत्र प्रत्ययैकतानता ध्यानम् ।।२।।

tatra pratyayaika-tānatā dhyānam

tatra there *pratyaya* attention, awareness *eka* one *tānatā* state of being directed, extension (*eka-tānatā* continuum) *dhyānam* meditation

Dhyāna is the continuous flow of awareness there. (2)

तदेवार्थमात्रनिर्भासं स्वरूपशून्यमिव समाधिः ।।३।।

tad evārtha-mātra-nirbhāsaṃ svarūpa-śūnyam iva samādhiḥ

tat that (object) *eva* indeed, verily *artha* aim, purpose, use *mātra* only, by itself *nirbhāsam* shining with, appearing *svarūpa* own nature *śūnyam* devoid *iva* as if *samādhiḥ* transcendence, even intellect

Samādhi is when that object becomes as if devoid of its own nature, and awareness appears by itself. (3)

त्रयमेकत्र संयमः ।।४।।

trayam ekatra saṃyamaḥ

trayam three (*dhāraṇā*, *dhyāna* and *samādhi*) *ekatra* in one, together *saṃyamaḥ* binding together

The three taken together are *saṃyama*. (4)

तज्जयात्प्रज्ञालोकः ॥५॥

taj-jayāt prajñālokaḥ

*ta*t that (*saṃyama*) *jayāt* through mastery *prajñā* complete wakefulness *ālokaḥ* splendor

Through mastery of *saṃyama*, the splendor of complete wakefulness dawns. (5)

तस्य भूमिषु विनियोगः ॥६॥

tasya bhūmiṣu viniyogaḥ

tasya of that (*saṃyama*) *bhūmiṣu* in stages *viniyogaḥ* application

The application of *saṃyama* is in stages. (6)

त्रयमन्तरङ्गं पूर्वेभ्यः ।।७।।

trayam antar-aṅgaṃ pūrvebhyaḥ

trayam three (*dhāraṇā, dhyāna* and *samādhi*) *antaḥ* inner, internal *aṅgam* limb *pūrvebhyaḥ* from the previous

Dhāraṇā, dhyāna and *samādhi* are internal limbs, compared to the previous. (7)

तदपि बहिरङ्गं निर्बीजस्य ।।८।।

tad api bahir-aṅgaṃ nirbījasya

tat that (*saṃyama*) *api* even, also *bahiḥ* outer, external *aṅgam* limb *nirbījasya* of the seedless, of unbounded awareness

Even *saṃyama* is an external limb of unbounded awareness. (8)

व्युत्थाननिरोधसंस्कारयोरभिभवप्रादुर्भावौ
निरोधक्षणचित्तान्वयो निरोधपरिणामः ॥९॥

vyutthāna-nirodha-saṃskārayor abhibhavaprādurbhāvau
nirodha-kṣaṇa-cittānvayo nirodhapariṇāmaḥ

vyutthāna manifest *nirodha* withheld *saṃskārayoḥ* between the impressions *abhibhava* disappearance *prādurbhāvau* appearance *nirodha* cessation, complete settling *kṣaṇa* moment *citta* mind *anvayaḥ* junction point, conjunction *nirodha* settling, cessation *pariṇāmaḥ* transformation, modification

The *nirodha* transformation of mind is at the junction point—the moment of complete settling between the disappearance of manifest impressions and appearance of withheld impressions. (9)

तस्य प्रशान्तवाहिता संस्कारात् ॥१०॥

tasya praśānta-vāhitā saṃskārāt

tasya of that (settling) *praśānta* calmness *vāhitā* flow, continuum *saṃskārā*t through impression, repeated experience

Through the repeated experience of settling, a continuum of calmness develops. (10)

सर्वार्थतैकाग्रतयोः क्षयोदयौ चित्तस्य समाधिपरिणामः ।।११।।

sarvārthataikāgratayoḥ kśayodayau cittasya samādhi-pariṇāmaḥ

sarva all, diversified *arthatā* objectness, diversity *ekāgratayoḥ* of unified awareness, one-pointedness *kśaya* collapse *udayau* in the rise *cittasya* of mind *samādhi* even intellect, transcendental consciousness *pariṇāmaḥ* transformation, modification

The *samādhi* transformation of mind is in the collapse of diversified awareness and the rise of unified awareness. (11)

ततः पुनः शान्तोदितौ तुल्यप्रत्ययौ
चित्तस्यैकाग्रतापरिणामः ॥१२॥

tataḥ punaḥ śāntoditau tulya-pratyayau
cittasyaikāgratā-pariṇāmaḥ

tataḥ then *punaḥ* again *śānta* settled, subsided *uditau* uprisen *tulya* same, equal *pratyayau* states *cittasya* of mind *ekāgratā* unified awareness, one-pointedness *pariṇāmaḥ* transformation

Then again comes unified awareness, the *ekāgratā* transformation of mind, in which subsided and uprisen states are the same. (12)

एतेन भूतेन्द्रियेषु धर्मलक्षणावस्थापरिणामा व्याख्याताः ॥१३॥

etena bhūtendriyeṣu dharma-lakṣaṇāvasthāpariṇāmā vyākhyātāḥ

etena by this *bhūta* element (objective creation) *indriyeṣu* in the senses (subjective creation) *dharma* characteristic *lakṣaṇa* temporal quality *avasthā* state *pariṇāmāḥ* modifications, transformations *vyākhyātāḥ* explained

By this are explained the transformations of the characteristics, temporal qualities and states in the entire objective and subjective creation. (13)

शान्तोदिताव्यपदेश्यधर्मानुपाती धर्मी ॥१४॥

śāntoditāvyapadeśya-dharmānupātī dharmī

śānta subsided (past) *udita* uprisen (present) *avyapadeśya* undefined (future) *dharma* characteristic *anupātī* succession, sequence *dharmī* bearer of characteristics, object

An object unfolds as a succession of past, present and future characteristics. (14)

क्रमान्यत्वं परिणामान्यत्वे हेतुः ॥१५॥

kramānyatvaṃ pariṇāmānyatve hetuḥ

krama sequence *anyatvam* difference, change *pariṇāma* modification, transformation *anyatve* in a difference, in a change *hetuḥ* cause

A change in sequence causes a change in transformations. (15)

परिणामत्रयसंयमादतीतानागतज्ञानम् ॥१६॥

pariṇāma-traya-saṃyamād-atītānāgata-jñānam

pariṇāma modification, transformation *traya* three *saṃyamāt* from binding together, from collected awareness *atīta* past *anāgata* future *jñānam* knowledge

From *saṃyama* on the three transformations comes knowledge of the past and future. (16)

शब्दार्थप्रत्ययानामितरेतराध्यासात्संकरस्
तत्प्रविभागसंयमात्सर्वभूतरुतज्ञानम् ।।१७।।

śabdārtha-pratyayānām itaretarādhyāsāt saṃkaras tat-pravibhāga-saṃyamāt sarva-bhūta-rutajñānam

śabda sound *arth*a object *pratyayānām* of ideas *itara* other *adhyāsāt* from the superimposition *saṃkaraḥ* confusion *tat* that (name, form and idea) *pravibhāga* distinction *saṃyamāt from* collected awareness *sarva* all *bhūta* living beings *ruta* sound *jñānam* knowledge

Confusion arises from the superimposition of sound, form and idea on one another. From *saṃyama* on their distinction comes knowledge of the sound of all living beings. (17)

संस्कारसाक्षात्करणात्पूर्वजातिज्ञानम् ।।१८।।

saṃskāra-sākṣāt-karaṇāt pūrva-jāti-jñānam

saṃskāra impression *sākṣāt* before the eyes *karaṇāt* from making (*sākṣāt-karaṇāt* from putting before the eyes, from perception) *pūrva* previous *jāti* birth *jñānam* knowledge

From perception of impressions comes knowledge of previous births. (18)

प्रत्ययस्य परचित्तज्ञानम् ।।१९।।

pratyayasya para-citta-jñānam

pratyayasya of a mental impulse, of attention *para* another *citta* mind *jñānam* knowledge

From a mental impulse comes knowledge
of another's mind. (19)

न च तत्सालम्बनं

तस्याविषयीभूतत्वात् ।।२०।।

na ca tat sālambanaṃ tasyāviṣayī-bhūtatvāt

na not *ca* and, but *tat* that (knowledge) *sa* with, including *ālambanam* support, basis, cause *tasya* of it (another's mind) *aviṣayī* no object (of perception) *bhūtatvāt* because there is, from there being

But that knowledge does not include the cause of another's thoughts, because their object of perception is not possible to know. (20)

कायरूपसंयमात्तद्ग्राह्यशक्तिस्तम्भे
चक्षुःप्रकाशासंप्रयोगेऽन्तर्धानम् ।।२१।।

kāya-rūpa-saṃyamāt tad-grāhya-śakti-stambhe
cakṣuḥ-prakāśāsaṃprayoge 'ntar-dhānam

kāya body *rūpa* form *saṃyamāt* through collected awareness *tat* that (the form of the body) *grāhya* to be grasped, to be perceived *śakti* ability, capability *stambhe* in disruption *cakṣuḥ* eye *prakāśa* appearance, illumination, light *asaṃprayoge* without contact *antaḥ-dhānam* invisibility

From *saṃyama* on the form of the body—when the ability to perceive that form is disrupted and there is no contact of its light with the eye—invisibility is gained. (21)

सोपक्रमं निरुपक्रमं च कर्म
तत्संयमादपरान्तज्ञानमरिष्टेभ्यो वा ॥२२॥

sopakramaṃ nirupakramaṃ ca karma
tat-saṃyamād aparānta-jñānam ariṣṭebhyo vā

sopakramam approach (quickly) *nirupakramam* without approach (slowly) *ca* and *karma* action, fruit of action *tat* that *saṃyamāt* from collected awareness *aparānta* the far end (death) *jñānam* knowledge *ariṣṭebhyaḥ* from premonitions *vā* or

Karma returns both quickly and slowly. From *saṃyama* on that, or from premonitions, comes knowledge of death. (22)

मैत्र्यादिषु बलानि ॥२३॥

maitry-ādiṣu balāni

maitrī friendliness *ādiṣu* and so on *balāni* strengths

Through *saṃyama* on friendliness, and so on, these qualities are strengthened. (23)

बलेषु हस्तिबलादीनि ।।२४।।

baleṣu hasti-balādīni

baleṣu on the strengths *hasti* elephant *bala* strength *ādīni* and so on

The strength of an elephant, and so on, is obtained through *saṃyama* on these strengths. (24)

प्रवृत्त्यालोकन्यासात्सूक्ष्मव्यवहितविप्रकृष्ट ज्ञानम् ।।२५।।

pravṛtty-āloka-nyāsāt sūkṣma-vyavahitaviprakṛṣṭa-jñānam

pravṛtti coming forth, appearance, manifestation *āloka* inner light, inner vision *nyāsāt* from directing, from applying, from bringing forth *sūkṣma* subtle *vyavahita* hidden *viprakṛṣṭa* distant *jñānam* knowledge

Knowledge is gained about what is subtle, hidden or distant by allowing the inner light to come forth. (25)

भुवनज्ञानं सूर्ये संयमात् ।।२६।।

bhuvana-jñānaṃ sūrye saṃyamāt

bhuvana universe, cosmos *jñānam* knowledge *sūrye* on the sun *saṃyamāt* through collected awareness

Through *saṃyama* on the sun comes knowledge of the universe. (26)

चन्द्रे ताराव्यूहज्ञानम् ।।२७।।

candre tārā-vyūha-jñānam

candre on the moon *tārā* star *vyūha* arrangement *jñānam* knowledge

Through *saṃyama* on the moon comes knowledge of the arrangement of the stars. (27)

ध्रुवे तद्गतिज्ञानम् ।।२८।।

dhruve tad-gati-jñānam

dhruve on the polestar (Polaris) *tat* that (the stars) *gati* movement *jñānam* knowledge

Through *saṃyama* on the polestar comes knowledge of the movement of the stars. (28)

नाभिचक्रे कायव्यूहज्ञानम् ।।२९।।

nābhi-cakre kāya-vyūha-jñānam

nābhi navel *cakre* on the center, on the plexus *kāya* body *vyūha* system, arrangement, structure *jñānam* knowledge

From *saṃyama* on the navel plexus, comes knowledge of the bodily systems. (29)

कण्ठकूपे क्षुत्पिपासानिवृत्तिः ।।३०।।

kaṇṭha-kūpe kṣut-pipāsā-nivṛttiḥ

kaṇṭha throat *kūpe* on the hollow *kṣut* hunger *pipāsā* thirst *nivṛttiḥ* subdued

Through *saṃyama* on the hollow of the throat, hunger and thirst are subdued. (30)

कूर्मनाड्यां स्थैर्यम् ।।३१।।

kūrma-nāḍyāṃ sthairyam

kūrma tortoise, bronchial tube, windpipe *nāḍyām* on the tube *sthairyam* calmness, steadiness

Through *saṃyama* on the bronchial tube,
calmness is gained. (31)

मूर्धज्योतिषि सिद्धदर्शनम् ।।३२।।

mūrdha-jyotiṣi siddha-darśanam

mūrdha head *jyotiṣi* on the light *siddha* perfected being *darśanam* vision

Through *saṃyama* on the light in the head comes vision of perfected beings. (32)

प्रातिभाद्वा सर्वम् ।।३३।।

prātibhād vā sarvam

prātibhāt through intuition *vā* or *sarvam* everything

Or through intuition everything can be known. (33)

हृदये चित्तसंवित् ।।३४।।

hṛdaye citta-saṃvit

hṛdaye on the heart *citta* mind *saṃvit* knowledge, understanding

Through *saṃyama* on the heart comes understanding of the mind. (34)

सत्त्वपुरुषयोरत्यन्तासंकीर्णयोः
प्रत्ययाविशेषो भोगः
परार्थत्वात्स्वार्थसंयमात्पुरुषज्ञानम् ॥३५॥

sattva-puruṣayor atyantāsaṃkīrṇayoḥ pratyayāviśeṣo bhogaḥ parārthatvāt svārthasaṃyamāt puruṣa-jñānam

sattva intellect (*buddhi*) *puruṣayoḥ* between the Self (*puruṣa*) *atyanta* absolute *asaṃkīrṇayoḥ* between the unmixed *pratyaya* experience *aviśeṣaḥ* no distinction *bhogaḥ* outer enjoyment *para* other (*puruṣa*) *arthatvāt* from the purposefulness *sva* own *artha* purpose *saṃyamāt* through collected awareness *puruṣa* Self *jñānam* knowledge

Outer enjoyment makes no distinction in the experience of *buddhi* and *puruṣa*—which are absolutely unmixed, because *buddhi* is purposeful to another and *puruṣa* is purposeful to itself. Through *saṃyama* on the distinction between *buddhi* and *puruṣa*, comes knowledge of *puruṣa*. (35)

ततः प्रातिभश्रावणवेदनादर्शास्वादवार्ता जायन्ते ।।३६।।

tataḥ prātibha-śrāvaṇa-vedanādarśāsvāda-vārtā jāyante

tataḥ from that (knowledge of *puruṣa*) *prātibha* intuition *śrāvaṇa* hearing *vedanā* touching *ādarśa* seeing, sight *āsvāda* taste *vārtāḥ* smell *jāyante* are born, arise

From knowledge of *puruṣa* arise intuition and refined hearing, touch, sight, taste and smell. (36)

ते समाधावुपसर्गा व्युत्थाने सिद्धयः ।।३७।।

te samādhāv upasargā vyutthāne siddhayaḥ

te these *samādhau* in transcendence *upasargāḥ* subordinate *vyutthḥne* in activity, in awakening *siddhayaḥ* perfections, accomplishments, proofs, supernormal powers

These are proofs of awakening and yet are subordinate in *samādhi*. (37)

बन्धकारणशैथिल्यात्प्रचारसंवेदनाच्च
चित्तस्य परशरीरावेशः ।।३८।।

bandha-kāraṇa-śaithilyāt pracāra-saṃvedanāc ca cittasya para-śarīrāveśaḥ

bandha bondage *kāraṇa* cause *śaithilyāt* through loosening *pracāra* movement, manifestation *saṃvedanāt* through perception *ca* and *cittasya* of the mind *para* other *śarīra* body *āveśaḥ* entering

Through loosening the cause of bondage and through perception of the movements of the mind, entering the body of another is possible. (38)

उदानजयाज्जलपङ्ककण्टकादिष्वसङ्ग
उत्क्रान्तिश्च ।।३९।।

udāna-jayāj jala-paṅka-kaṇṭakādiṣv asaṅga utkrāntiś ca

udāna upward breath (responsible for speech, memory, etc.) *jayāt* through mastery *jala* water *paṅka* mud *kaṇṭaka* thorn *ādiśu* and so forth *asaṅgaḥ* non-contact *utkrāntiḥ* rising up *ca* and

Through mastery of the upward breath, *udāna*, comes freedom from contact with water, mud, thorns, etc., and the ability to rise up. (39)

समानजयाज्ज्वलनम् ।।४०।।

samāna-jayāj jvalanam

samāna even breath (responsible for digestion, etc.) *jayāt* through mastery *jvalanam* effulgence, radiance

Through mastery of the even breath, *samāna*, effulgence is gained. (40)

श्रोत्राकाशयोः संबन्धसंयमाद्दिव्यं श्रोत्रम् ।।४१।।

śrotrākāśayoḥ saṃbandha-saṃyamād divyaṃ śrotram

śrotra ear, hearing *ākāśayoḥ* between space *saṃbandha* relationship, connection *saṃyamāt* through collected awareness *divyam* divine *śrotram* ear, hearing

Through *saṃyama* on the relationship between hearing and *ākāśa*, divine hearing is gained. (41)

कायाकाशयोः संबन्धसंयमाल्लघुतूलसमापत्तेश्चाकाश-गमनम् ॥४२॥

kāyākāśayoḥ saṃbandha-saṃyamāl laghu-tūlasamāpatteś cākāśa-gamanam

kāya body *ākāśayoḥ* between space *saṃbandha* relationship *saṃyamāt* through collected awareness *laghu* lightness *tūla* cotton fiber *samāpatteḥ* through absorption *ca* and *ākāśa* space *gamanam* movement

Through *saṃyama* on the relationship between the body and *ākāśa* and through absorption in the lightness of cotton fiber, movement through space is gained. (42)

बहिरकल्पिता वृत्तिर्महाविदेहा ततः प्रकाशावरणक्षयः ॥४३॥

bahir akalpitā vṛttir mahā-videhā tataḥ prakāśāvaraṇa-kṣayaḥ

bahiḥ external *akalpitā* unimagined *vṛttiḥ* mental activity *mahā* great *videhā* bodiless state *tataḥ* through that *prakāśa* inner light *āvaraṇa* covering *kṣayaḥ* dissolved

Mental activity which is external to the body and unimagined is called the "great bodiless state." Through that, the covering over inner light is dissolved. (43)

स्थूलस्वरूपसूक्ष्मान्वयार्थवत्त्वसंयमाद्
भूतजयः ।।४४।।

sthūla-svarūpa-sūkṣmānvayārthavattva-saṃyamād bhūtajayaḥ

sthūla gross form (earth, water, fire, air, space) *svarūpa* essence (hardness, liquidity, heat, mobility, all-pervasiveness) *sūkṣma* subtle form (smell, taste, form, texture, sound) *anvaya* connectedness, association, relationship (*sāttvika, rājasika, tāmasika*) *arthavattva* purposefulness (toward or away from *kaivalya*) *saṃyamāt* through collected awareness *bhūta* element *jayaḥ* mastery

Mastery over the elements is gained through *saṃyama* on the gross form, essence, subtle form, connectedness and purposefulness of an object. (44)

ततोऽणिमादिप्रादुर्भावः
कायसंपत्तद्धर्मानभिघातश्च ।।४५।।

tato 'ṇimādi-prādurbhāvaḥ
kāya-saṃpat tad-dharmānabhighātaś ca

tataḥ from that (mastery) *aṇima* minuteness *ādi* and so on *prādurbhāvaḥ* arisen, manifestation *kāya* body *saṃpat* perfection *tat* that (body) *dharma* characteristic *anabhighātaḥ* indestructibility *ca* and

From that arises the ability to become minute and so on, perfection of the body and indestructibility of its characteristics. (45)

रूपलावण्यबलवज्रसंहननत्वानि
कायसंपत् ।।४६।।

rūpa-lāvaṇya-bala-vajra-saṃhananatvāni kāya-saṃpat

rūpa handsome form, beauty *lāvaṇya* grace *bala* strength *vajra* diamond, thunderbolt *saṃhananatvāni* firmness, strength, compactness *kāya* body *saṃpat* perfection

Perfection of the body consists of beauty, grace, strength and the firmness of a diamond. (46)

ग्रहणस्वरूपास्मितान्वयार्थवत्त्वसंयमाद्
इन्द्रियजयः ।।४७।।

grahaṇa-svarūpāsmitānvayārthavattva-saṃyamād indriya-jayaḥ

grahaṇa grasping, ability to perceive *svarūpa* own form, essence *asmitā* individuality *anvaya* connectedness *arthavattva* purposefulness *saṃyamāt* through collected awareness *indriya* sense *jayaḥ* mastery

Mastery over the senses is gained through *saṃyama* on their ability to perceive, their essence, individuality, connectedness and purposefulness. (47)

ततो मनोजवित्वं विकरणभावः
प्रधानजयश्च ।।४८।।

tato mano-javitvaṃ vikaraṇa-bhāvaḥ pradhāna-jayaś ca

tataḥ from that (mastery) *manaḥ* mind *javitvam* swiftness *vikaraṇa* without instrument, without a physical structure *bhāvaḥ* being, existence *pradhāna* source, nature *jayaḥ* mastery *ca* and

From that comes movement as swift as the mind, existence without a physical structure and mastery over nature. (48)

सत्त्वपुरुषान्यताख्यातिमात्रस्य सर्वभावाधिष्ठातृत्वं सर्वज्ञातृत्वं च ।।४९।।

sattva-puruṣānyatā-khyāti-mātrasya
sarva-bhāvādhiṣṭhātṛtvaṃ sarva-jñātṛtvaṃ ca

sattva intellect (*buddhi*) *puruṣa* Self *anyatā* distinction *khyāti* perception *mātrasya* only, solely *sarva* all *bhāva* existence *adhiṣṭātṛtvam* supremacy *sarva* all *jñātṛtvam* knowingness *ca* and

Solely from perception of the distinction between *buddhi* and *puruṣa* comes all-knowingness and supremacy over all that exists. (49)

तद्वैराग्यादपि दोषबीजक्षये कैवल्यम् ।।५०।।

tad-vairāgyād api doṣa-bīja-kṣaye kaivalyam

tat that (all-knowingness and supremacy) *vairāgyāt* through non-attachment *api* even *doṣa* suffering, defect, deficiency, imbalance *bīja* seed, source *kṣaye* in the collapse *kaivalyam* singularity, enlightenment

Through non-attachment even to that—when the source of imbalance has collapsed—there is singularity, *kaivalya*. (50)

स्थान्युपनिमन्त्रणे सङ्गस्मयाकरणं
पुनरनिष्ठप्रसङ्गात् ।।५१।।

sthāny-upanimantraṇe saṅga-smayākaraṇaṃ
punar aniṣṭa-prasaṅgāt

sthāni well-established, celestial being *upanimantraṇe* on the invitation *saṅga* attachment *smaya* pride *akaraṇam* no cause *punaḥ* again *aniṣṭa* undesirable *prasaṅgāt* because of the ocurrence of a possibility

There is no cause for attachment or pride upon invitation from those who are well-established, because the undesirable may occur again. (51)

क्षणतत्क्रमयोः संयमाद्विवेकजं ज्ञानम् ।।५२।।

kṣaṇa-tat-kramayoḥ saṃyamād vivekajaṃ jñānam

kṣaṇa moment *tat* it *kramayoḥ* on the sequences *saṃyamāt* through collected awareness *vivekajam* discrimination-born *jñānam* knowledge

Through *saṃyama* on a moment and its sequence, discriminative knowledge is born. (52)

जातिलक्षणदेशैरन्यतानवच्छेदात्तुल्ययोस्
ततः प्रतिपत्तिः ।।५३।।

jāti-lakṣaṇa-deśair anyatānavacchedāt tulyayos tataḥ pratipattiḥ

jāti species *lakṣaṇa* characteristic, temporal appearance *deśaiḥ* by position *anyatā* difference, distinction *anavacchedāt* from no separation *tulyayoḥ* of two similars *tataḥ* then *pratipattiḥ* ability to discriminate

Then comes the ability to discriminate between objects that seem similar—indistinguishable by species, characteristic or position. (53)

तारकं सर्वविषयं सर्वथाविषयमक्रमं चेति
विवेकजं ज्ञानम् ।।५४।।

tārakaṃ sarva-viṣayaṃ sarvathā-viṣayam akramaṃ ceti vivekajaṃ jñānam

tārakam liberating *sarva* all *viṣayam* object *sarvathā* all times *viṣayam* object *akramam* without sequence, holistic *ca* and *iti* thus *vivekajam* discrimination-born *jñānam* knowledge

This knowledge born of discrimination is liberating and holistic—it includes all objects and all times. (54)

सत्त्वपुरुषयोः शुद्धिसाम्ये कैवल्यम् ।।५५।।

sattva-puruṣayoḥ śuddhi-sāmye kaivalyam

sattva intellect (*buddhi*) *puruṣayoḥ* of the Self *śuddhi* purity *sāmye* in equality *kaivalyam* singularity, enlightenment

When *buddhi* becomes as pure as *puruṣa*, enlightenment dawns. (55)

Kaivalya-Pāda

Chapter on Enlightenment

जन्मौषधिमन्त्रतपःसमाधिजाः सिद्धयः ।।१।।

janmauṣadhi-mantra-tapaḥ-samādhi-jāḥ siddhayaḥ

janma birth *auṣadhi* herbs *mantra* instrument of thought *tapaḥ* abstainment, purification *samādhi* transcendence *jāḥ* born, arise *siddhayaḥ* perfections, attainments

Siddhis arise through birth, herbs, *mantra,*
tapas or *samādhi.* (1)

जात्यन्तरपरिणामः प्रकृत्यापूरात् ।।२।।

jāty-antara-pariṇāmaḥ prakṛty-āpūrāt

jāti form of existence *antara* another *pariṇāmaḥ* transformation *prakṛti* nature *āpūrāt* from abundance, from filling up

Transformation into another form of existence comes from the abundance of nature. (2)

निमित्तमप्रयोजकं प्रकृतीनां वरणभेदस्तु ततः क्षेत्रिकवत् ।।३।।

nimittam aprayojakaṃ prakṛtīnāṃ varaṇa-bhedas tu tataḥ kṣetrikavat

nimittam apparent cause, efficient cause *aprayojakam* not the cause *prakṛtīnām* of natural changes *varaṇa* enclosing, obstacle *bhedaḥ* removal *tu* but *tataḥ* in this *kṣetrikavat* like a farmer (who channels water for crops by removing barriers)

The apparent cause of natural change is not the real cause, but rather the removal of an obstacle. In this it is like a farmer who channels water for crops by removing barriers. (3)

निर्माणचित्तान्यस्मितामात्रात् ।।४।।

nirmāṇa-cittāny asmitā-mātrāt

nirmāṇa creating *cittāni* minds *asmitā* individuality *mātrāt* from solely

Minds are created solely from individuality. (4)

प्रवृत्तिभेदे प्रयोजकं चित्तमेकमनेकेषाम् ॥५॥

pravṛtti-bhede prayojakaṃ cittam ekam anekeṣām

pravṛtti activity *bhede* in diverse *prayojakam* cause *cittam* mind *ekam* one *anekeṣām* of many (minds)

The one mind is the cause of many minds engaged in diverse activities. (5)

तत्र ध्यानजमनाशयम् ॥६॥

tatra dhyāna-jam anāśayam

tatra there, of these (minds) *dhyāna* meditation *jam* produced, born *anāśayam* free from impressions

Of these minds, the one produced through meditation is free from impressions. (6)

कर्माशुक्लाकृष्णं योगिनस्त्रिविधमितरेषाम् ।।७।।

karmāśuklākṛṣṇaṃ yoginas tri-vidham itareṣām

karma action *aśukla* not white *akṛṣṇam* not black *yoginaḥ* of a *yogi* *trividham* threefold *itareṣām* of others

The action of a *yogi* is neither white nor black, while of others it is threefold. (7)

ततस्तद्विपाकानुगुणानामेवाभिव्यक्तिर् वासनानाम् ।।८।।

tatas tad-vipākānuguṇānām evābhivyaktir vāsanānām

tataḥ from that (action) *tat* that (action) *vipāka* fruit *anuguṇānām* of similar qualities *eva* exactly, very *abhivyaktiḥ* creation, manifestation *vāsanānām* of mental impressions

Action creates mental impressions which have very similar qualities to the fruit of that action. (8)

जातिदेशकालव्यवहितानामप्यानन्तर्यं
स्मृतिसंस्कारयोरेकरूपत्वात् ।।९।।

jāti-deśa-kāla-vyavahitānām apy ānantaryaṃ
smṛti-saṃskārayor eka-rūpatvāt

jāti birth *deśa* place *kāla* time *vyavahitānām* separated, concealed *api* even *ānantaryam* successive relation *smṛti* memory *saṃskārayoḥ* of impressions *eka* one *rūpatvāt* from the form (*eka-rūpatvāt* from the uniformity)

Because of the uniformity of memory and impression, an action and its mental impressions are related, even when separated by birth, place and time. (9)

तासामनादित्वं चाशिषो नित्यत्वात् ।।१०।।

tāsām anāditvaṃ cāśiṣo nityatvāt

tāsām of those (impressions) *anāditvam* beginningless *ca* and *āśiṣaḥ* of desire *nityatvāt* because of the perpetual nature

And those impressions are beginningless because of the perpetual nature of desire. (10)

हेतुफलाश्रयालम्बनैः
संगृहीतत्वादेषामभावे तदभावः ॥११॥

hetu-phalāśrayālambanaiḥ
saṃgṛhītatvād eṣām abhāve tad-abhāvaḥ

hetu cause (ignorance) *phala* fruit (effort) *āśraya* substratum (mind) *ālambanaiḥ* by the objects (of perception) *saṃgṛhītatvāt* from binding, from bondage *eṣām* of these *abhāve* in the absence *tat* that (impression) *abhāvaḥ* absence

Ignorance, effort, mind and object are bound together. When these disappear, mental impressions disappear. (11)

अतीतानागतं स्वरूपतोऽस्त्यध्व-
भेदाद्धर्माणाम् ॥१२॥

atītānāgataṃ svarūpato 'sty adhva-bhedād dharmāṇām

atīta past *anāgatam* not yet come (future) *svarūpataḥ* in essence, in reality *asti* exists *adhva* course, development *bhedāt* because of the difference *dharmāṇām* of characteristics

Past and future exist in reality because of the difference in the development of characteristics. (12)

ते व्यक्तसूक्ष्मा गुणात्मानः ।।१३।।

te vyakta-sūkṣmā guṇātmānaḥ

te these (characteristics) *vyakta* manifest *sūkṣmāḥ* subtle *guṇa* quality *ātmānaḥ* composed of, nature

These characteristics have qualities of a manifest or subtle nature. (13)

परिणामैकत्वाद्वस्तुतत्त्वम् ।।१४।।

pariṇāmaikatvād vastu-tattvam

pariṇāma transformation *ekatvāt* from the uniformity, from the continuity *vastu* object *tattvam* essential nature

The essential nature of an object is found from the uniformity of transformation. (14)

वस्तुसाम्ये चित्तभेदात्तयोर्विभक्तः पन्थाः ।।१५।।

vastu-sāmye citta-bhedāt tayor vibhaktaḥ panthāḥ

vastu object *sāmye* in sameness *citta* mind *bhedāt because* of the diversity *tayoḥ* of the two (object and knowledge about it) *vibhaktaḥ* distinction *panthāḥ* path

Though an object is the same, because minds are diverse, the path of an object and the knowledge about it are distinct. (15)

न चैकचित्ततन्त्रं वस्तु तदप्रमाणकं तदा किं स्यात् ।।१६।।

na caika-citta-tantraṃ vastu tad-apramāṇakaṃ tadā kiṃ syāt

na not *ca* and *eka* one, single *citta* mind *tantram* dependent *vastu* object *tat* that (mind) *apramāṇakam* not valid knowledge, not perceivable *tadā* then, for in that case *kim* what *syāt* would become

And an object does not depend upon a single mind. For in that case what would become of it when not perceived by that mind? (16)

तदुपरागापेक्षित्वाच्चित्तस्य वस्तु ज्ञाताज्ञातम् ।।१७।।

tad-uparāgāpekṣitvāc cittasya vastu jñātājñātam

tat it (the object) *uparāga* coloring, influence *apekṣitvāt* depending upon *cittasya* of the mind *vastu* object *jñāta* known *ajñātam* not known

An object is known or not known, depending upon whether it influences the mind. (17)

सदा ज्ञाताश्चित्तवृत्तयस्तत्प्रभोः पुरुषस्यापरिणामित्वात् ।।१८।।

sadā jñātāś citta-vṛttayas tat-prabhoḥ puruṣasyāpariṇāmitvāt

sadā always *jñātāḥ* known *citta* mind *vṛttayaḥ* activities *tat* it (mind) *prabhoḥ* of the basis, of the superior *puruṣasya* of consciousness *apariṇāmitvāt* because of the nonchange

The activity of the mind is always known, because consciousness, its basis, does not change. (18)

न तत्स्वाभासं दृश्यत्वात् ।।१९।।

na tat svābhāsaṃ dṛśyatvāt

na not *tat* it (mind) *svābhāsam* self-luminous *dṛśyatvāt* because of being perceivable

The mind is not self-luminous, because it is perceivable. (19)

एकसमये चोभयानवधारणम् ।।२०।।

eka-samaye cobhayānavadhāraṇam

eka one *samaye* in coming together (*eka-samaye* at the same time) *ca* and *ubhaya* both (mind and object) *anavadhāraṇam* non-cognition

And it is not possible to cognize both the mind and its object at the same time. (20)

चित्तान्तरदृश्ये बुद्धिबुद्धेरतिप्रसङ्गः
स्मृतिसंकरश्च ।।२१।।

cittāntara-dṛśye buddhi-buddher atiprasaṅgaḥ
smṛti-saṃkaraś ca

citta mind *antara* another *dṛśye* in the seeing *buddhi* intellect *buddheḥ* of intellect *atiprasaṅgaḥ* over-occurance *smṛti* memory *saṃkaraḥ* confusion *ca* and

If the mind was seen by another mind, there would be an over-occurrence of intellect observing intellect and confusion of memory. (21)

चित्तेरप्रतिसंक्रमायास्तदाकारापत्तौ
स्वबुद्धिसंवेदनम् ।।२२।।

citter apratisaṃkramāyās tad-ākārāpattau
sva-buddhi-saṃvedanam

citteḥ of consciousness *apratisaṃkramāyāḥ* unmoving, unmixed *tat* that (intellect) *ākāra* form *āpattau* in assuming *sva* own *buddhi* intellect *saṃvedanam* knowledge, perception

Consciousness, though unmoving, gains knowledge of its own intellect by assuming its form. (22)

द्रष्टृदृश्योपरक्तं चित्तं सर्वार्थम् ।।२३।।

draṣṭṛ-dṛśyoparaktaṃ cittaṃ sarvārtham

draṣṭṛ knower *dṛśya* known *uparaktam* colored, influenced *cittam* mind *sarva* all *artham* comprehensive

The mind, influenced by knower and known, is all-comprehensive. (23)

तदसंख्येयवासनाभिश्चित्रमपि परार्थं संहत्यकारित्वात् ।।२४।।

tad asaṃkhyeya-vāsanābhiś citram api parārthaṃ saṃhatya-kāritvāt

tat that (mind) *asaṃkhyeya* innumerable *vāsanābhiḥ* with impressions *citram* variety *api* though *para* other (*puruṣa*) *artham* purpose, sake *saṃhatya* association *kāritvāt* because of activity

The mind, though having an innumerable variety of impressions, exists for the sake of *puruṣa*, because it acts in association with it. (24)

विशेषदर्शिन आत्मभावभावनाविनिवृत्तिः ।।२५।।

viśeṣa-darśina ātma-bhāva-bhāvanā-vinivṛttiḥ

viśeṣa distinctness (of *puruṣa*) *darśinaḥ* of the seer, for one who has cognized *ātma* Self *bhāva* nature *bhāvanā* reflection *vinivṛttiḥ* cessation

For one who has cognized the distinctness of *puruṣa*, reflection about the nature of the Self ceases. (25)

तदा विवेकनिम्नं कैवल्यप्राग्भारं चित्तम् ।।२६।।

tadā viveka-nimnaṃ kaivalya-prāgbhāraṃ cittam

tadā then *viveka* discrimination *nimnam* inclined toward *kaivalya* singularity *prāgbhāram* not far from, inclined *cittam* mind

Then the mind is inclined toward discrimination and is not far from *kaivalya*. (26)

तच्छिद्रेषु प्रत्ययान्तराणि संस्कारेभ्यः ।।२७।।

tac-chidreṣu pratyayāntarāṇi saṃskārebhyaḥ

tat that (state) *chidreṣu* in the gaps, in the intervals *pratyaya* thought *antarāṇi* other *saṃskārebhyaḥ* due to impressions

In the gaps in that state, other thoughts arise due to impressions. (27)

हानमेषां क्लेशवदुक्तम् ।।२८।।

hānam eṣāṃ kleśavad uktam

hānam removal *eṣām* of these *kleśavat* like affliction *uktam* is said

The removal of these is said to be like the removal of afflictions. (28)

प्रसंख्यानेऽप्यकुसीदस्य सर्वथा
विवेकख्यातेर्धर्ममेघः समाधिः ॥२९॥

prasaṃkhyāne 'py akusīdasya sarvathā
viveka-khyāter dharma-meghaḥ samādhiḥ

prasaṃkhyāne in absorption, in reflection *api* even *akusīdasya* of one who has no gain, no interest *sarvathā* continuous, constant *viveka* discrimination *khyāteḥ* of one with awareness, vision *dharma* natural law *meghaḥ* cloud *samādhiḥ* transcendence

For one who has nothing to gain even in the deepest absorption, who has continuous discriminative awareness, *dharma megha samādhi* is gained. (29)

ततः क्लेशकर्मनिवृत्तिः ॥३०॥

tataḥ kleśa-karma-nivṛttiḥ

tataḥ from that (*dharma megha samādhi*) *kleśa* affliction, cause of suffering *karma* action, the binding influence of action *nivṛttiḥ* removal

From that comes the removal of afflictions and the binding influence of action. (30)

तदा सर्वावरणमलापेतस्य
ज्ञानस्यानन्त्याज्ज्ञेयमल्पम् ।।३१।।

tadā sarvāvaraṇa-malāpetasya jñānasyānantyāj jñeyam alpam

tadā then *sarva* all *āvaraṇa* obstruction, covering *mala* impurity *apetasya* of the removal *jñānasya* of knowledge *ānantyāt* because of the infinity *jñeyam* to be known *alpam* little

Then—because knowledge is infinite when all obstructing impurities are removed—little remains to be known. (31)

ततः कृतार्थानां
परिणामक्रमसमाप्तिर्गुणानाम् ।।३२।।

tataḥ kṛtārthānāṃ
pariṇāma-krama-samāptir guṇānām

tataḥ then *kṛta* done, fulfilled *arthānām* of the purposes *pariṇāma* transformation *krama* sequence *samāptiḥ* end, completion *guṇānām* of nature

Then nature has fulfilled its purpose and the sequence of transformations is complete. (32)

क्षणप्रतियोगी
परिणामापरान्तनिर्ग्राह्यः क्रमः ॥३३॥

kṣaṇa-pratiyogī pariṇāmāparānta-nirgrāhyaḥ kramaḥ

kṣaṇa moment *pratiyogī* being dependent upon *pariṇāma* change, transformation, evolution *apara* final, nothing beyond *anta* end *nirgrāhyaḥ* liberated, released *kramaḥ* sequence, course, succession

Sequence, which depends upon moments, is liberated at the final end of transformations. (33)

पुरुषार्थशून्यानां गुणानां प्रतिप्रसवः कैवल्यं स्वरूपप्रतिष्ठा वा चितिशक्तिरिति ।।३४।।

puruṣārtha-śūnyānāṃ guṇānāṃ pratiprasavaḥ kaivalyaṃ svarūpa-pratiṣṭhā vā citi-śaktir iti

puruṣa Self *artha* purpose *śūnyānām* devoid, absence *guṇānām* of the activities of nature *pratiprasavaḥ* return to original state, reabsorption *kaivalyam* singularity, enlightenment *svarūpa* own nature *pratiṣṭhā* establishment *vā* or *citi* awareness, consciousness *śaktiḥ* infinite power, ability, dynamism, faculty *iti* the end

In the absence of activity, the purpose of *puruṣa* is fulfilled, and what remains is *kaivalya*—the infinite power of consciousness established in its own nature. (34)

Lightning Source UK Ltd.
Milton Keynes UK
UKOW030010191212

203830UK00001B/143/P

9 781421 891323